BUILDING THE TITANIC

Jodie Shepherd

Children's Press®
An imprint of Scholastic Inc.

Content Consultant
Tim Maltin, *Titanic* author and historian

Library of Congress Cataloging-in-Publication Data
Names: Shepherd, Jodie, author.
Title: Building the Titanic/Jodie Shepherd.
Other titles: True book.
Description: First edition. | New York: Children's Press, an imprint of Scholastic Inc., 2022. | Series: A true
    book | Includes bibliographical references and index. | Audience: Ages 8–10. | Audience: Grades 4–6.
    | Summary: "Next set in A TRUE BOOK series. Young readers rediscover the story of the largest and
    most luxurious ship ever built, The Titanic. Featuring historical imagery, first-hand accounts, and lively
    text"—Provided by publisher.
Identifiers: LCCN 2022002398 (print) | LCCN 2022002399 (ebook) | ISBN 9781338840476 (library binding)
    | ISBN 9781338840483 (paperback) | ISBN 9781338840490 (ebk)
Subjects: LCSH: Titanic (Steamship)—Juvenile literature. | Titanic (Steamship)—Design and construction—
    Juvenile literature. | Ocean liners—Design and construction—Juvenile literature.
Classification: LCC G530.T6 S476 2022 (print) | LCC G530.T6 (ebook) | DDC 623.82/432—dc23/
    eng/20220221
LC record available at https://lccn.loc.gov/2022002398
LC ebook record available at https://lccn.loc.gov/2022002399

10 9 8 7 6 5 4 3 2 1   23 24 25 26 27

Printed in China 62
First edition, 2023

Design by Kathleen Petelinsek
Series produced by Spooky Cheetah Press

**Front cover: The *Titanic* under construction at
Harland & Wolff shipyard; (top) the ship's propellers;
(bottom) workers stand near the anchor chain**

Back cover: Workers install rivets in the *Titanic*'s hull.

Find the Truth!

Everything you are about to read is true *except* for one of the sentences on this page.

Which one is **TRUE**?

T or F   There were four huge smokestacks on the *Titanic*, but only three of them worked.

T or F   The *Titanic* was powered by 200 coal-burning boilers.

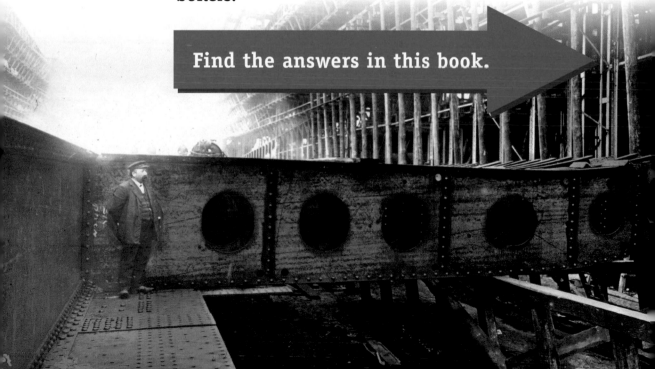

Find the answers in this book.

What's in This Book?

The **BIG** Truth

The *Titanic* sank less
than three hours after
hitting an iceberg.

Why Did People Think the *Titanic* Was Unsinkable?

This is a reproduction of the *Titanic*'s Grand Staircase.

3 Fitting Out the Ship

4 A Floating Hotel

Thousands of people showed up to watch the *Titanic* leave the shipyard.

Building the World's Most Famous Ship

Most people have heard of the ship called the *Titanic* and the tragic tale of its sinking on the night of **April 14–15, 1912,** after hitting an iceberg. The story is famous around the world. But history is filled with shipwrecks, including some that had a much greater loss of life. **So why are people still fascinated by the *Titanic*, more than 100 years after it sank?**

The *Titanic* was **world-famous** long before it set sail. After all, the *Titanic* and its twin ship, the *Olympic*, were the **largest** ships ever built at the time. And the **most luxurious**.

Southampton, England

New York City

U.S.

ATLANTIC OCEAN

Where the *Titanic* sank

Many people believed that the *Titanic* could not sink. But it did—on its very first voyage. Ever since that fateful night, the *Titanic*'s story has continued to grow in people's imagination. **This is the story of how—and why—the *Titanic* was built.**

Sailing ships like this one relied on the wind. If the weather was too calm, the ship could not move.

A Bold Plan

In the eighteenth century, ships that traveled on the ocean had sails. They depended on wind to move them. In 1838, the *Sirius* became the first ship powered entirely by steam to cross the Atlantic Ocean. Steam engines work by burning large amounts of coal or wood. Over time, ship engines grew stronger and more **efficient**. Soon there were many shipping companies that carried passengers, goods, and even mail across the ocean.

A book called *Futility* was published 10 years before the *Titanic's* voyage. The book was about a ship named *Titan* that hit an iceberg and sank.

Passengers line the docks near the *Teutonic*.

Star of the Sea

By 1889, the White Star Line, which later built the *Titanic*, was one of the biggest shipping companies in the world. That year it **launched** the first modern **ocean liners** the world had ever seen: *Teutonic* and *Majestic*. The two new ships were enormous compared with any that had come before. White Star ships quickly became known for their size, as well as for their **luxury**.

Between 1900 and 1915, more than 15 million immigrants, like those pictured here, arrived in the United States.

A New Travel Option

The White Star Line offered some of the most luxurious third-class, or **steerage**, accommodations. Steerage was the least expensive way to travel across the Atlantic. Millions of **emigrants** were fleeing poverty and hardship in Europe. They hoped to make a fresh start in America. But they didn't have money to pay for very expensive rooms. White Star could afford to sell cheap steerage tickets and also offer them comfortable accommodations and good food.

Titanic Plans Begin

The Cunard Line was another large shipping company. In 1907, Cunard finished work on two new ships: *Lusitania* and *Mauretania*. They were the biggest and fastest ships yet. How could the White Star Line ever compete? That question would be answered at a dinner party at Lord Pirrie's house in London. Lord Pirrie was a partner at Harland and Wolff, one of the largest shipyards in the world. Pirrie's dinner guest was J. Bruce Ismay, the White Star Line's managing director.

Pirrie (left) and Ismay (right). Ismay was on the *Titanic*'s doomed voyage. He survived.

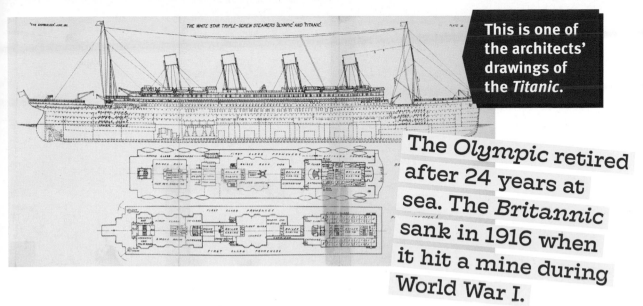

THE WHITE STAR TRIPLE-SCREW STEAMERS OLYMPIC AND TITANIC.

This is one of the architects' drawings of the *Titanic*.

The *Olympic* retired after 24 years at sea. The *Britannic* sank in 1916 when it hit a mine during World War I.

The World's Biggest Ships

Pirrie and Ismay decided to build three new ships. It would not be efficient to build ships that could go faster than the new Cunard ships. Instead, they would build the biggest, most luxurious ships in the world, with the most up-to-date technology. Even the ships' names would be large: *Titanic*, *Olympic*, and *Gigantic*. (*Gigantic* was later changed to the more patriotic name of *Britannic*.) The men began sketching ideas for their ships that very night.

The gantries used to build the *Titanic* were the largest in the world. They could be seen all over Belfast, Ireland.

This postcard shows the *Titanic* under construction.

Building Begins

Construction began on both the *Titanic* and the *Olympic* at the Harland and Wolff shipyards in Belfast, Ireland, in March 1909. The **slipway** near the water had to be made large enough to hold both ships. Opposite the docks, the River Lagan had to be dug deeper so the ships wouldn't hit the bottom as they journeyed to the ocean. Building equipment had to be extra-large, too. Two enormous new gantries, or metal frames, were constructed over the slipway. They would be used to support huge cranes and other machinery.

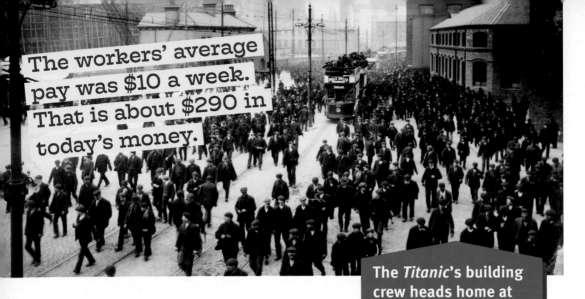

The workers' average pay was $10 a week. That is about $290 in today's money.

The *Titanic*'s building crew heads home at the end of a work day.

At the Docks

Thousands of men from nearby Belfast neighborhoods were hired for the White Star project. They worked on all the different parts of the *Titanic*. Many workers did specialized jobs, such as carpentry, electrical work, and plumbing. Other workers were unskilled, which simply meant they had no specialized training. Most of these unskilled laborers worked as riveters. Their job was to join together the giant steel plates that made up the body of the ship, using fasteners called rivets.

Hard at Work

Almost 4,000 workers helped build the *Titanic*. And it was not an easy job! Workers labored six days a week, from early morning until early evening. They were given just eight days of unpaid holiday a year: one week off in summer, as well as Christmas Day and Easter. Workers were fined for damaged tools and for breaking rules on the job site, including being late to work. The workplace was dangerous, like all shipyards at the time. Accidents were common. Eight workers died during the building of the *Titanic*, and about 250 were injured.

A worker stands next to one of the *Titanic*'s giant steel beams.

The Ship's Skeleton

The *Titanic* was built from the bottom up. First came the keel, the ship's long spine. That beam ran from the ship's front (called the bow) to its back (stern). More beams were laid on each side, and more were laid across, from one side of the ship to the other. Then workers built up the curved outer frame, or **hull**, of the ship. Long beams ran across the ship at each level, to hold up the *Titanic*'s 10 decks.

The keel is placed in position at the shipyard.

The *Titanic*'s biggest plates weighed more than four tons each. That is almost as heavy as an adult hippo!

More than three million rivets held the *Titanic* together!

When the ship's skeleton was finished, riveters covered the *Titanic*'s entire hull with steel plates to make it completely **watertight**. Teams of workers would heat up the rivets and push them through two metal plates at a time. Then the rivets were hammered into place to join the plates.

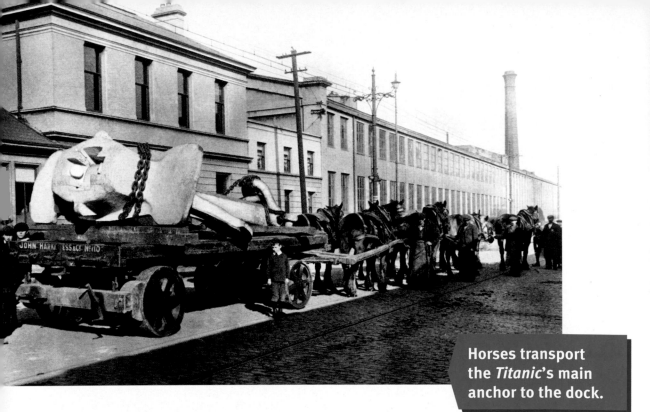

Ready to Launch

The *Titanic* was mostly finished on the outside, but inside, it was still an empty shell. The ship was ready to be moved to another spot, where its interior would be added. The *Titanic* was finally headed for the water! But first, the ship would need several anchors. The ship's main anchor was so heavy that it took 20 horses to pull the wagon that brought it to the dock.

Into the Water

On May 31, 1911, the *Titanic* was launched from the slipway into the water. The platform was greased, oiled, and soaped in order to make the ship's voyage from the docks smooth. It is estimated that around 100,000 people showed up to watch. The spectators crowded into the shipyard and along the banks of the river. They did not want to miss the exciting event! It took just over a minute for the *Titanic* to slip into the water.

The *Titanic* was as long as 22 city buses.

A crowd gathers to watch the *Titanic* enter the water for the first time.

21

Why Did People Think the *Titanic* Was Unsinkable?

The ship had the most advanced engineering features known to builders at that time. Here are two of those special features: the *Titanic*'s double hull and watertight compartments.

Double Hull

In the 1900s, ships' hulls were made with one layer of steel. The *Titanic* had a double hull at the bottom, near the keel. The double floors of steel meant the ship's bottom was extra strong.

Double hull —————

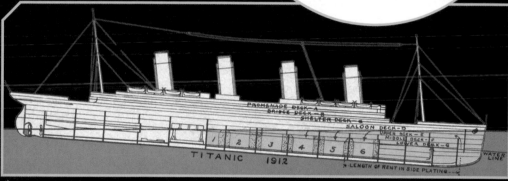

Watertight Compartments

The hull was divided into 16 watertight compartments, which were separated by steel walls called **bulkheads**. The compartments were designed to shut tight and stay sealed if the ship started flooding. The ship would stay afloat, even if the front four compartments filled with water.

The *Titanic*'s state-of-the-art design was not enough to save it: When the *Titanic* struck the iceberg, five compartments were damaged. The *Titanic* was not designed to cope with that amount of underwater damage. As the compartments filled with water, the ship sank lower and more water spilled over the tops of the bulkheads. The ship could no longer stay afloat.

The *Titanic's* fitting-out took about 10 months.

A tugboat guides the *Titanic* down the River Lagan. Tugboats are used to tow or push large ships.

Fitting Out the Ship

Once the *Titanic* was floating, five tugboats towed it to a human-made lake known as a basin to get "fitted out." Fitting out a ship means constructing its insides. The first step for the *Titanic* was adding the machinery that would make the ship run. Fitting-out also included putting in windows, or portholes; building the cabins, common rooms, kitchens, and staircases; and bringing in the furniture and decorations—everything that would prepare the ship for passengers.

Each boiler was the size of a three-story house!

A huge floating crane, like the one shown here with the *Olympic*, was needed to move the *Titanic*'s giant parts.

Steam Power

The machinery needed to make the *Titanic* run was built at the same time the hull was under construction. Those items were built in factories and then shipped to Belfast. They included 24 boilers, which would power the ship; three bronze propellers, which would move it through the water; and a rudder, which was used for steering. When the *Titanic*'s fitting-out began, installing the ship's 24 huge boilers was one of the first jobs. A giant floating crane lifted the boilers into place.

Boilers at Work

The *Titanic* was powered by steam—and boilers were the key to that process. Enormous piles of coal were shoveled into the boilers' furnaces to make fires. The fires heated the water at the top of the boilers, turning it to steam, which then traveled through pipes to the ship's steam engines. The engines turned the enormous propellers that made it possible for the ship to travel quickly. They also powered turbines to make electricity, refrigeration, and heating possible on the ship.

These reproductions of the *Titanic*'s boilers are in a museum in England. The photo at right shows the *Titanic*'s actual boilers.

Up in Smoke

The enormous amount of coal that powered the *Titanic* created a lot of smoke. Three giant funnels, or smokestacks, were added to the ship to remove the soot. A fourth, at the back of the ship, was mostly for show! Lord Pirrie had decided that the *Titanic* would look even more impressive with four funnels instead of three. That was to make the ship look elegant and also to appeal to those passengers who felt that large ships with four funnels were safer than smaller ships with fewer funnels!

The fourth smokestack was as big as the others. Besides being there for show, it also provided ventilation.

At the time of the *Titanic*'s trip, many people didn't even have electricity in their homes yet.

This is a reproduction of a stateroom on the *Titanic*.

Light It Up!

Electricians installed miles and miles of wiring so that the ship would have electricity. In the *Titanic*'s most expensive cabins, there were electric heaters, electric lamps, and electric bells for requesting help from the crew. There were also four elevators on board.

No photos of the *Titanic's* staircase have survived. The existing photos are from her twin ship, the *Olympic*.

This reproduction of the Grand Staircase is in a museum in Australia.

A Floating Hotel

The *Titanic* was famous for its size, but it was probably the ship's fancy design that really caught people's attention. One example was the Grand Staircase, which connected seven of the ship's 10 decks. There was a glass-and-iron dome above the staircase to let in light during the day. There were gold-covered crystal chandeliers to light it up at night. Passengers on the *Titanic* traveled in different classes: first, second, and third. Not all the accommodations were this fancy, but everything about the ship was impressive, even in third class.

The *Titanic* was one of the first ships with a heated swimming pool.

First Class: Pure Luxury

Accommodations for first-class passengers were placed near the ship's top. The cabins were in the middle of the ship, where it was quieter and where passengers were less likely to get seasick. Passengers had a choice of areas and restaurants, including the Café Parisien, which was built to look like a sidewalk cafe straight from Paris. A library, a gym, a heated swimming pool, and a spa area were also built for first-class passengers. The spa area had cold plunge pools and steam and massage rooms.

Second Class: Near Luxury

Second-class passengers would also live in luxury while on board. Like the first-class travelers, they could stroll along the promenade deck. Only one second-class dinning room was built, but it was elegant and would feature live music. This class also had its own library, barbershop, and men-only smoking rooms. Cabins were large and comfortable. However, second-class passengers would have to share bathrooms!

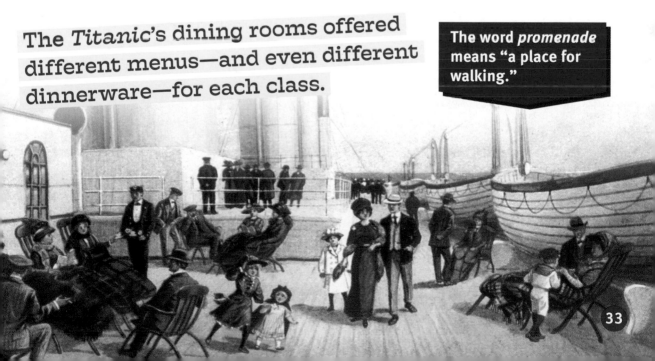

The *Titanic*'s dining rooms offered different menus—and even different dinnerware—for each class.

The word *promenade* means "a place for walking."

33

Third Class: Inexpensive, but Comfortable

More than half the ship's passengers traveled in third class. However, even they would enjoy more luxury than they were used to. Steerage cabins were located toward the bottom and stern of the ship, near the engine room. The cabins had bunk beds, and unmarried passengers would room with strangers of the same gender. But every cabin had electric heat, lights, and sinks with running water. Steerage had its own dining room and lounge. Travelers would be able to relax there with music— provided by their fellow passengers—and dancing.

The third-class sitting room was not fancy, but it was comfortable.

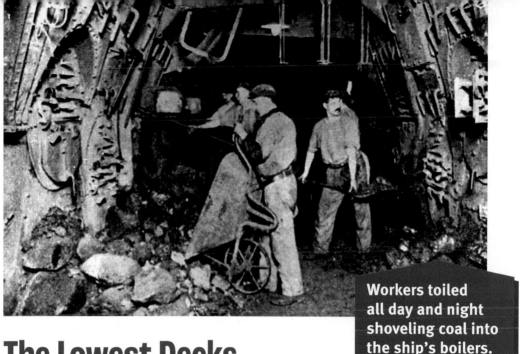

Workers toiled all day and night shoveling coal into the ship's boilers.

The Lowest Decks

The tank top was the ship's lowest deck. The engine rooms, boiler rooms, and rooms for storing coal, known as bunkers, were located in this part of the ship. The freshwater tanks that supplied passengers with drinking water were located here, too. The propellers that would help speed the ship along ran through this deck and then out through the back of the ship. The orlop deck was one deck up. That was where the ship's food and luggage were stored, along with millions of pieces of mail.

Captain Smith had been a professional sailor for 40 years. He went down with the ship.

The Command Center

The *Titanic*'s top deck was called the boat deck, and it housed the ship's command center, which is called the bridge. Here, the *Titanic*'s captain, Edward John Smith, would keep watch and give orders to steer. He could also communicate with crew and passengers in other parts of the ship. Smith and his top officers would also have living quarters on this deck. The promenade area for first- and second-class passengers was on the boat deck, too. So was the first-class gym. Two features of the boat deck would become very important once the *Titanic* hit the iceberg: the radio communications room and lifeboat storage.

Lack of Lifeboats

The *Titanic* did not have enough lifeboats for its passengers and crew. Many people have wondered why. In 1912, the law required that ships carry just 16 lifeboats. But then, no one had ever imagined a ship as big as the *Titanic*! At different times in the planning, up to 64 lifeboats were included for the *Titanic*. Because so many boats were not required by law, though, the ship carried much fewer. In the end, the *Titanic*'s 16 wooden lifeboats, plus four **collapsible** lifeboats, weren't nearly enough to save everyone when the ship hit the iceberg.

Passengers stroll past some of the *Titanic*'s wooden lifeboats.

It's a Date!

The date for the *Titanic*'s first voyage was supposed to be March 20, 1912, but it had to be pushed back. The *Olympic*, which was already at sea, had gotten into an accident. The *Olympic*'s repairs had to come first. The *Titanic*'s new sailing date would be April 10. After three years, it was time for the *Titanic*'s final touches. Three enormous bronze propellers were installed. Then the ship was placed in dry dock briefly for a last coat of paint.

Timeline: Life of the *Titanic*

1907
The idea for the *Titanic* is born at a dinner party.

1909
Building begins at the Harland and Wolff shipyard in Belfast, Ireland.

1910
The keel is completed and the plating of the hull begins.

1911
The *Titanic* moves from the slipway into the water.

Full Speed Ahead

Before the *Titanic* could begin its first voyage, the ship had to be tested at sea. Top speed was measured. Anchors were dropped, then raised again. The ship was made to turn in a complete circle at high speed. Could the *Titanic*'s engines be stopped and started at sea? How long did it take to make an emergency stop? Did the radios work? The *Titanic* passed every test. The crew and passengers could finally come aboard. They had no way of knowing the tragedy that lay ahead.

March 31, 1912
Construction and fitting-out of the *Titanic* is complete, inside and out.

April 2, 1912
The *Titanic* is put through its sea trials and passes easily.

April 10, 1912
The *Titanic* sets sail on its first—and only—voyage.

April 14–15, 1912
The *Titanic* strikes an iceberg and sinks in the North Atlantic.

Discovered Parts

We learn about the past through primary sources. These include objects or written materials that were created at the time of the event being studied. The wreck of the *Titanic* was discovered in 1985. Since then, many parts of the ship have been photographed and others have been brought to the surface, giving us evidence of how the ship was put together and what it looked like when finished. Check out some of the parts that were found!

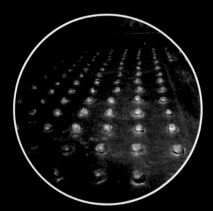

Hull

This is one of the largest recovered pieces of the hull from the *Titanic*. Notice the rows and rows of rivets!

Porthole

There were more than 2,000 portholes on the ship. This one is a window from a third-class cabin.

The Bow

This photograph of the *Titanic*'s bow was taken at the wreck site. It is still underwater.

Hot and Cold Water

Every cabin on the *Titanic* had running water. The first-class cabins had both hot- and cold-water valves.

Stained Glass Window

This decorative window was one of several found in first-class areas of the ship.

Propeller

This is one of the *Titanic*'s two wing propellers. The ship also had a center propeller.

The *Titanic*'s Engineering Features in Place

Smokestacks

Three giant funnels removed the smoke and soot coming from the boilers. The fourth was for ventilation—and for show.

Stern

Underwater View

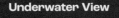

Rudder

This huge metal piece was used to steer the ship. The *Titanic*'s rudder was nearly identical to the rudder shown here, which is from the *Olympic*.

Propellers

Steam power from the engines turned the propellers, making it possible for the ship to travel quickly through the water.

Engines

The *Titanic* was powered by two giant steam engines. Each one was 30 feet (9 meters) tall.

Main Anchor

The main anchor was stored in the bow of the ship. A large **winch** was used to lower the anchor into the water and haul it back up.

Bow

Boilers

Day and night, workers shoveled coal into the enormous boilers. The burning coal created steam.

Double Hull

Made of giant steel plates, the double-layered hull was designed to make the bottom of the ship especially strong and doubly watertight.

Rivets

Millions of short metal pins, known as rivets, were used to join the hull's steel plates.

True Statistics

Ship's length: 882.9 feet (269.1 m) long

Ship's width: more than 92 feet (28 m) wide

Ship's weight: over 92 million pounds (42 million kg)

Number of portholes: more than 2,000

Number of people it could carry when filled: up to 3,547

Number of masts: 2, but they were used for navigation lights and flags, not for sails

Cost of building the *Titanic*: more than $7 million (close to $400 million in today's money)

Did you find the truth?

(T) There were four huge smokestacks on the *Titanic*, but only three of them worked.

(F) The *Titanic* was powered by 200 coal-burning boilers.

Resources

Other books in this series:

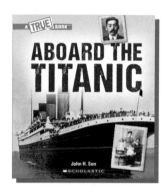 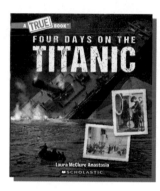 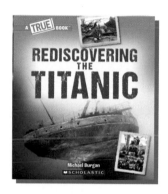

You can also look at:

Brewster, Hugh, and Laurie Coulter. *882½ Amazing Answers to Your Questions about the Titanic*. New York: Scholastic/Madison Press, 1998.

Callery, Sean. *Titanic: A Picture History of the Shipwreck That Shocked the World*. New York: Scholastic, 2014.

Green, Rod. *Building the Titanic: An Epic Tale of the Creation of History's Most Famous Ocean Liner*. Pleasantville, NY: Reader's Digest, 2005.

McCollum, Sean. *Building the Titanic: The Making of a Doomed Ship*. North Mankato, MN: Capstone Press, 2015.

Glossary

bulkheads (BUHLK-hedz) upright structures or partitions designed to resist pressure or to shut off water

collapsible (kuh-LAP-suh-buhl) capable of being folded into a small space

efficient (i-FISH-uhnt) working very well and not wasting time or energy

emigrants (EM-i-gruhntz) people who leave one country to settle in another

hull (huhl) the frame or body of a boat or ship

launched (lawncht) set a boat or ship afloat, especially if it has just been built

luxury (LUHK-shur-ee) something expensive that is nice to have but that you do not really need

ocean liners (OH-shuhn LYE-nurz) ships that run on a regular schedule from one seaport to another

slipway (SLIP-way) a sloping surface that leads into the water and is used to build, launch, or repair boats or ships

steerage (STEER-ij) the section of a ship where lower-paying passengers stay

watertight (WAH-tur-tite) completely sealed so that water cannot enter or leave

winch (winch) a machine that lifts or pulls heavy objects

Index

Page numbers in **bold** indicate illustrations.

About the Author

Jodie Shepherd, who also writes under the name Leslie Kimmelman, is the author of more than 75 fiction and nonfiction children's books. She is also a former children's book editor. Shepherd has been on a sea voyage only once, and it was memorable—aboard a ship in the Alaskan waterway. She recently visited the *Titanic* museum in Halifax, Nova Scotia. It was fascinating!